# THE JESUS ADVENTURE

STUDY GUIDE

Copyright © 2024 by Ian Millar

Published by Kudu Publishing

All rights reserved. No portion of this book may be reproduced, stored in a retrieval system, or transmitted in any form or by any means—electronic, mechanical, photocopy, recording, scanning, or other—except for brief quotations in critical reviews or articles, without prior written permission of the author.

Unless otherwise specified, all Scripture quotations are taken from the Contemporary English Version (CEV), copyright © 1995 by American Bible Society. | Scripture quotations marked NIV are taken from the Holy Bible, New International Version®, NIV®. Copyright © 1973, 1978, 1984, 2011 by Biblica, Inc.™ Used by permission of Zondervan. All rights reserved worldwide. www.zondervan.com. The "NIV" and "New International Version" are trademarks registered in the United States Patent and Trademark Office by Biblica, Inc.™ | Scripture quotations marked NKJV are taken from the New King James Version®. Copyright © 1982 by Thomas Nelson. Used by permission. All rights reserved.

For foreign and subsidiary rights, contact the author.

Cover design by Sara Young
Cover photo by Naomi Steel

ISBN: 978-1-960678-21-8     1 2 3 4 5 6 7 8 9 10

Printed in the United States of America

# IAN MILLAR

# THE JESUS ADVENTURE

JOURNEY TO SPIRITUAL FREEDOM

**STUDY GUIDE**

# CONTENTS

CHAPTER 1. **SCOUTING THE WAY** ....................................................................8

CHAPTER 2. **COMMENCING THE ADVENTURE** ...........................................14

CHAPTER 3. **THE ADVENTURE WAY** ............................................................20

CHAPTER 4. **THE VITAL CURE** .....................................................................28

CHAPTER 5. **THE VOYAGE CHARTS OF PROVIDENCE** ..............................34

CHAPTER 6. **CROSSING OVER BY FAITH** .....................................................40

CHAPTER 7. **REST AND REFRESHMENT (ON THE WAY)** ...........................48

CHAPTER 8. **ADVENTURE OUTWARD: THE PRIME DIRECTIVE** .................54

CHAPTER 9. **EQUIPPED WITH SPIRITUAL WEAPONS** ................................60

CHAPTER 10. **SUPPLYING EARTH'S NEEDS FROM HEAVEN'S RESOURCES** .............68

CHAPTER 11. **CROSS WALKERS OF A NEW IDENTITY** ...............................74

CHAPTER 12. **THE TREASURE CHEST OF CHRIST** ......................................80

PART 1

# STARTING IN THE WAY OF JESUS

CHAPTER 1

# SCOUTING THE WAY

Jesus promises a hope and a future. Not because we're good but because He is good.

## READING TIME

As you read Chapter 1: "Scouting the Way" in *The Jesus Adventure*, review, reflect on, and respond to the text by answering the following questions.

# REVIEW, REFLECT, AND RESPOND

This chapter describes Jesus as the "faithful Scout" who goes before us. Why is this meaningful as you think about who Jesus has been to you in your own life?

_____

_____

_____

_____

_____

_____

_____

_____

The author mentions that Jesus came from "obscurity" but gained profound influence. How can this insight apply to how we think about our own influence or mission in life?

_____

_____

_____

_____

_____

_____

_____

_____

_____

The author states that Jesus came from the Father's throne in Heaven to the womb of a poor woman and became part of humanity. What does this say about His desire to know you intimately?

_____

_____

_____

_____

_____

_____

_____

_____

> *"We will know that we have come to know Jesus if we do His teachings."*
>
> —1 John 2:3 (author paraphrase)

*Consider the scripture above and answer the following questions:*

How does applying Jesus's teachings reveal Jesus to us?

_____

_____

_____

_____

_____

_____

How is this scripture a conditional promise?

The author mentions the modern misconception that "knowing about" Jesus is synonymous with "knowing Him by doing." How do you differentiate between knowing about Jesus and truly following Him in your daily life?

The concept of adventure is central in this chapter. How do you think Jesus's call to discipleship can be understood as a spiritual adventure rather than a routine? Does following Jesus ever feel like a routine to you? Why?

What obstacles do you face when trying to live out the adventurous, abundant life Jesus promises? How do the principles discussed in this chapter equip you to overcome them?

_____

_____

_____

_____

_____

In the story of Jesus calling His disciples, they left everything behind to follow Him. What might God be calling you to leave behind in your own life to more fully follow Him?

_____

_____

_____

_____

_____

The author uses the metaphor of "adventure boots" for stepping out in faith more boldly. Do you own a pair of "adventure boots," and how often do you put them on? What holds you back?

_____

_____

_____

_____

_____

CHAPTER 2

# COMMENCING THE ADVENTURE

If we start anywhere else, then
we start with confusion.

## READING TIME

As you read Chapter 2: "Commencing the Adventure" in *The Jesus Adventure,* review, reflect on, and respond to the text by answering the following questions.

# REVIEW, REFLECT, AND RESPOND

This chapter emphasizes Jesus's friendships with ordinary, flawed people. How is this aspect of Jesus a call to adventure? In what ways have you put God in a box as to whom He is willing and able to rescue?

_____

_____

_____

_____

_____

_____

_____

_____

Think about a time when your map was turned in the wrong direction. What happened, and what did you learn? What did you learn about God that enabled you to realign with His plan?

_____

_____

_____

_____

_____

_____

_____

_____

_____

THE JESUS ADVENTURE: STUDY GUIDE | 15

Jesus's invitation is simple: turn to God and believe the Good News. What areas of your life need this simplicity, and how can you "turn back to God" today?

_____

_____

_____

_____

_____

_____

_____

_____

> *"Call to me and I will answer you and tell you great and unsearchable things you do not know."*
>
> —Jeremiah 33:3 (NIV)

*Consider the scripture above and answer the following questions:*

What kind of "unsearchable" things has God revealed to your heart when you've called on Him?

_____

_____

_____

_____

_____

_____

_____

Why do you think God waits for us to call on Him before He shares what He knows with us?

The chapter discusses Jesus turning the focus away from rituals to relationships. Do you ever feel yourself departing from relationship and erring toward rituals? What kind of warning signs have you observed that signal you are on your way there, and how could you begin to hedge against it?

What are some of the "old gear" or past beliefs that you need to let go of in order to start fresh in your walk with God?

_____

_____

_____

_____

_____

_____

_____

Why can't we be complete until we turn to Jesus? What does it mean to be "complete"? Are you "complete"? Why or why not?

_____

_____

_____

_____

_____

_____

_____

What promises of God have been most impactful for you, and how have you acted on them? In what ways have you failed to act on them in the past?

_____

_____

_____

_____

_____

_____

_____

CHAPTER 3

# THE ADVENTURE WAY

He is not just offering to take us on
an adventure; He is the adventure.

## READING TIME

As you read Chapter 3: "The Adventure Way" in *The Jesus Adventure*, review, reflect on, and respond to the text by answering the following questions.

# REVIEW, REFLECT, AND RESPOND

The chapter discusses Jesus's call to follow Him. What does it look like to truly follow Him, and how have you followed Him today?

_____

_____

_____

_____

_____

_____

_____

Jesus told His apprentices that knowing Him comes from applying His teachings. Which teaching do you find difficult to walk out? How can you practically apply one of His teachings this week to draw closer to Him?

_____

_____

_____

_____

_____

_____

_____

_____

_____

_____

Jesus's actions and miracles are described as capturing the imagination. How does reflecting on His miracles help you grow in faith and trust in His power?

_____

_____

_____

_____

_____

_____

_____

_____

> *"Follow Me, and I will make you fishers of men."*
> —Matthew 4:19 (NKJV)

*Consider the scripture above and answer the following questions:*

How do you interpret Jesus's invitations to become "fishers of men"? Who in your life needs Jesus, and what steps can you take to become a fisherman?

_____

_____

_____

_____

_____

_____

_____

_____

What unique talents do you have that can help others see Christ through you, and how might they be used as "fishing gear"?

How do you sense Jesus inviting you to join in His adventure? What is holding you back from fully accepting that invitation?

How do you feel about the risks of following Jesus? Do they intimidate you? Do they deter you from going all in? Do they excite you? Explain.

What costs have you incurred from following Jesus? What makes it worth the cost?

Jesus's life fulfilled over three hundred prophecies. How does the fulfillment of prophecy impact your confidence in the reliability of Scripture?

The author states that Jesus wants people to discover who He is by learning and doing what He teaches. Which teachings of His have you put into action, and what new things have you discovered about Him as a result?

# PART 2

# WALKING THE WAY OF JESUS

CHAPTER 4

# THE VITAL CURE

> Everything God calls us to do seems wrong, yet it works. Everything that seems right ultimately fails.

## READING TIME

As you read Chapter 4: "The Vital Cure" in *The Jesus Adventure*, review, reflect on, and respond to the text by answering the following questions.

# REVIEW, REFLECT, AND RESPOND

This chapter highlights Jesus's compassion in healing. What areas of your life need healing? Who in your life have you witnessed Jesus heal, and how does it impact your faith in Him to heal you too?

_____

_____

_____

_____

_____

_____

_____

_____

Jesus's power to transform lives is emphasized in this chapter. In what ways have you experienced or witnessed transformation through following Him? Did it look the way you expected it to, and how does that add to the adventure?

_____

_____

_____

_____

_____

_____

_____

_____

_____

Have you allowed Jesus to explore and reveal the things hidden from your awareness that need healing? Have you allowed Jesus to heal those things that you know need healing but might be fearful to face?

---

---

---

---

---

---

> *"Moved with compassion, Jesus stretched out His hand and touched him, and said to him, 'I am willing; be cleansed!'"*
>
> —Luke 5:13 (author paraphrase)

*Consider the scripture above and answer the following questions:*

In this scripture, the leper asks Jesus if He would be willing to heal Him. Do you question Jesus's willingness to heal you? Why or why not? How could you bring this struggle to Jesus today?

---

---

---

---

---

---

---

What does it feel like to be "cleansed" by Jesus?

The chapter discusses the power Jesus has over sickness and sin. How do you see these two connected in your own life?

In what ways can you be an agent of Jesus's healing to those around you?

How can you focus on healing in your spiritual walk with Jesus in the next season of your life?

_____

_____

_____

_____

_____

_____

_____

_____

_____

_____

_____

_____

The chapter reflects on Jesus healing spiritual brokenness. How have you seen God work to heal you spiritually? Describe what happened.

_____

_____

_____

_____

_____

_____

_____

_____

_____

_____

_____

The author references the account of the crippled man who was lowered through the roof to be healed, but Jesus knew what he really needed was forgiveness and healing of his soul. What about this is meaningful for you as it relates to your own life?

_____

_____

_____

_____

_____

_____

_____

_____

_____

_____

This chapter highlights humility as an important component for receiving healing. Why is humility such an essential part of receiving from Jesus?

_____

_____

_____

_____

_____

_____

_____

_____

_____

_____

_____

_____

CHAPTER 5

# THE VOYAGE CHARTS
# OF PROVIDENCE

Jesus wants us to know how to
understand and to listen correctly.

## READING TIME

As you read Chapter 5: "The Voyage Charts of Providence" in *The Jesus Adventure*, review, reflect on, and respond to the text by answering the following questions.

# REVIEW, REFLECT, AND RESPOND

What does God's providence mean, in your own words?

_____

_____

_____

_____

_____

What does it mean to you that God has "charted" a course for your life? How much do you trust that plan?

_____

_____

_____

_____

_____

_____

_____

Think of a time when you experienced God's providence. How does that help you navigate current uncertainties?

_____

_____

_____

_____

_____

_____

_____

**THE JESUS ADVENTURE:** STUDY GUIDE | 35

> *"Here is the bread that comes down from heaven, which anyone may eat and not die. I am the living bread that came down from heaven. Whoever eats this bread will live forever. This bread is my flesh, which I will give for the life of the world."*
>
> —John 6:51 (author paraphrase)

*Consider the scripture above and answer the following questions:*

Why does Jesus refer to Himself as the "the living bread"? What does this symbolize?

_____

_____

_____

_____

_____

_____

_____

What does eating the living bread have to do with listening to and doing His Word? How hungry are you?

_____

_____

_____

_____

_____

_____

_____

_____

In what unexpected ways has God revealed Himself to you as you've listened to His guidance on your journey?

The chapter speaks about surrendering control to God's plans. Do you find it difficult to surrender to God? What areas of your life do you need to surrender more fully?

How do you discern God's guidance in making major life decisions? How do you know whether you are leading or God is leading?

Reflect on a time when God's plan differed from your own. What was that experience like, and what did you learn as you look back on that time?

How well do you recognize God's guiding hand in your everyday life? How sensitive are you to His leading?

How do you reconcile knowing that God's plans for you are good when your circumstances don't reflect it? How does listening to God mitigate the tension between your knowledge of His promises and your reality?

CHAPTER 6

# CROSSING OVER BY FAITH

Many people started to follow Jesus but gave up when it became uncomfortable or inconvenient. Others want to start, but only if they can squeeze God into their plans.

## READING TIME

As you read Chapter 6: "Crossing Over by Faith" in *The Jesus Adventure*, review, reflect on, and respond to the text by answering the following questions.

# REVIEW, REFLECT, AND RESPOND

How would you rate your faith on a scale from 1 to 5 (1 = no faith at all, 5 = a lot of faith)? Explain your reasoning behind that rating.

| 1 | 2 | 3 | 4 | 5 |
|---|---|---|---|---|

_____

_____

_____

_____

_____

_____

_____

_____

Reflect on a time when you had to walk by faith and not by sight. What were you seeing, and how did God work in that circumstance? What was the end result?

_____

_____

_____

_____

_____

_____

_____

_____

_____

Reflecting on the concept of "crossing over," what role has faith played in helping you transition from one season of life to another?

_____

_____

_____

_____

_____

_____

_____

> *"Now faith is the confidence in what we hope for and assurance about what we do not see."*
>
> **—Hebrews 11:1 (NIV)**

*Consider the scripture above and answer the following questions:*

How does this definition of faith challenge the way you approach unseen circumstances?

_____

_____

_____

_____

_____

_____

_____

_____

How much confidence do you have in something you are hoping for right now? Explain your answer.

In what ways did Jesus model crossing over by faith? What story in Scripture stands out to you the most, and why does it resonate with you?

The author describes moments when faith leads to breakthrough. How has faith led to breakthroughs in your own life?

**THE JESUS ADVENTURE:** STUDY GUIDE | 43

What role do timing and waiting play in the practice of crossing over by faith? Why do you think God makes us wait?

_____

_____

_____

_____

_____

_____

_____

_____

_____

_____

List three things God has done in your life that you never thought were possible. What does this teach you about the deficiency of your own strength to change your heart and circumstances?

_____

_____

_____

_____

_____

_____

_____

_____

_____

_____

Does faith come easily to you? Why or why not?

In what ways did this chapter challenge you? What principles will you begin to apply in your own life when you are tempted to doubt?

PART 3

# STANDING FIRM WITH JESUS

CHAPTER 7

# REST AND REFRESHMENT (ON THE WAY)

God gives us rest as a gift, so
we should gratefully use it.

## READING TIME

As you read Chapter 7: "Rest and Refreshment (On the Way)" in *The Jesus Adventure*, review, reflect on, and respond to the text by answering the following questions.

# REVIEW, REFLECT, AND RESPOND

This chapter emphasizes rest as a crucial part of the Jesus adventure. How do you make room for rest in your life? What do you do, and is it working?

_____

_____

_____

_____

_____

Reflect on a time when making time for rest was difficult. What could you have done differently to prioritize rest?

_____

_____

_____

_____

_____

In what areas of your life do you feel spiritually and emotionally drained? How can you seek refreshment from Jesus in those areas?

_____

_____

_____

_____

_____

> *"Come to me, all you who are weary and heavy laden, and I will give you rest."*
>
> —Matthew 11:28 (NKJV)

*Consider the scripture above and answer the following questions:*

Jesus promises rest for the weary. What burdens are you carrying that you need to bring to Him for rest?

_____

_____

_____

_____

_____

_____

_____

_____

What does it look like and feel like to receive Jesus's rest? How can you experience His rest and endure the storms of life at the same time?

_____

_____

_____

_____

_____

_____

_____

_____

_____

Do you set aside a Sabbath rest in your week? If so, what benefits have you noticed from that commitment? If not, what would a Sabbath look like for you and your family?

Jesus models balance between action and rest. What does this balance look like practically, and how can you better model this balance in your own life?

Reflect on a time when you experienced spiritual refreshment. What contributed to that, and how can you recreate those moments?

How does your perspective in periods of rest differ from your perspective during periods of chaos and distress? What kind of narratives do you find yourself rehearsing in each scenario?

---

What distractions or habits might be preventing you from entering into rest? What could you eliminate from your life that may be robbing you of the rest you need?

---

Jesus calls us to rest in Him. How does this challenge the demands of the fast-paced, achievement-driven culture around us? How can you counteract that in your life?

CHAPTER 8

# ADVENTURE OUTWARD: THE PRIME DIRECTIVE

He isn't sending angels to our friends and families. He's sending us.

## READING TIME

As you read Chapter 8: "Adventure Outward: The Prime Directive" in *The Jesus Adventure*, review, reflect on, and respond to the text by answering the following questions.

# REVIEW, REFLECT, AND RESPOND

The chapter discusses taking the adventure outward by reaching others. How have you been challenged to share your faith with those around you?

_____

_____

_____

_____

_____

The prime directive of following Jesus involves mission and outreach. In what ways have you participated in outreach?

_____

_____

_____

_____

How has your story made a difference in someone else's life? Whose story has impacted you, and how does that inspire you to share your story with more people?

_____

_____

_____

_____

_____

> *"You are like light for the whole world. A city built on top of a hill cannot be hidden."*
>
> —Matthew 5:14 (CEV)

*Consider the scripture above and answer the following questions:*

In what ways might you be "hiding" the light that God has given you?

_____

_____

_____

_____

_____

_____

_____

How does the image of a "city on a hill" encourage you to live out your faith in a way that is visible and impactful to others?

_____

_____

_____

_____

_____

_____

_____

_____

What fears or obstacles prevent you from sharing your faith with others?

Who in your life do you feel is in need of hope? Who needs to hear your testimony?

How can you become more mission-minded in the places you go every day, seeing your workplace, neighborhood, or school as a mission field?

How has being on mission for God deepened your faith or broadened your understanding of the world?

Reflect on a time when you ignored God's nudge to step out and share your faith with someone else. What held you back?

Craft a short personal testimony of how God changed your life through the death and resurrection of Jesus Christ, and ask God to send you someone whose heart has been prepared to hear it.

CHAPTER 9

# EQUIPPED WITH SPIRITUAL WEAPONS

When we really grasp who He is and what He is saying to us, we begin to fathom the power of His name.

## READING TIME

As you read Chapter 9: "Equipped with Spiritual Weapons" in *The Jesus Adventure*, review, reflect on, and respond to the text by answering the following questions.

# REVIEW, REFLECT, AND RESPOND

The chapter discusses spiritual weapons for battling darkness. How equipped do you feel to fight spiritual battles, and what weapons do you need to wield?

_____

_____

_____

_____

_____

_____

In what areas of your life do you feel spiritually vulnerable, and how can you better protect yourself with the weapons God provides?

_____

_____

_____

_____

_____

What does it look like practically to fight dark, spiritual forces rather than flesh and blood?

_____

_____

_____

_____

_____

**THE JESUS ADVENTURE:** STUDY GUIDE | 61

> *"Put on the full armor of God, so that you can take your stand against the devil's schemes."*
>
> —Ephesians 6:11 (NIV)

*Consider the scripture above and answer the following questions:*

What part of the armor of God do you feel you most need to strengthen? Why?

_____

_____

_____

_____

_____

_____

_____

_____

What schemes of the enemy have you experienced? How have you responded to them in the past, and how can you respond differently now?

_____

_____

_____

_____

_____

_____

_____

_____

How does the chapter's emphasis on spiritual battles affect how you view the challenges you face in life?

What practical steps can you take to be more aware of spiritual warfare in your everyday life?

The chapter discusses the sword of the Spirit which is God's Word. How can you use Scripture to fight your battles and prepare yourself for attacks?

Meditate on prayer as a spiritual battle strategy. Why is the enemy so threatened by prayer?

_____

_____

_____

_____

_____

_____

_____

_____

_____

_____

The chapter emphasizes standing firm. What does standing firm look like in the context of your current life situation?

_____

_____

_____

_____

_____

_____

_____

_____

_____

_____

_____

PART 4

# SEATED WITH JESUS

CHAPTER 10

# SUPPLYING EARTH'S NEEDS FROM HEAVEN'S RESOURCES

We discover that God always gives more to the givers. If there is something you lack, give it away.

## READING TIME

As you read Chapter 10: "Supplying Earth's Needs from Heaven's Resources" in *The Jesus Adventure*, review, reflect on, and respond to the text by answering the following questions.

# REVIEW, REFLECT, AND RESPOND

What does it mean to use Heaven's resources to meet the needs of the Earth?

_____

_____

_____

_____

_____

_____

What role does the body of Christ play in bringing Heaven's resources to supply the Earth's needs?

_____

_____

_____

_____

_____

How do you feel called to act as a conduit of Heaven's resources? What can you give to others, even if you don't have much of it yourself?

_____

_____

_____

_____

_____

**THE JESUS ADVENTURE:** STUDY GUIDE | 69

> *"One person gives freely, yet gains even more; another withholds unduly, but comes to poverty. A generous person will prosper; whoever refreshes others will be refreshed."*
>
> —Proverbs 11:24-25 (NIV)

*Consider the scripture above and answer the following questions:*

Explain the differences between the world's economy and God's economy described in this verse. Why do you think God designed the kingdom to operate this way?

_____

_____

_____

_____

_____

_____

_____

What generally holds you back from giving freely?

_____

_____

_____

_____

_____

_____

_____

Reflect on a time when you gave freely without expecting anything in return. How did that experience impact you? How did it challenge you?

In what ways is God supplying your daily needs? How can you become more attuned to the ways He meets your needs day to day?

The chapter emphasizes that God's provision often goes beyond material needs. How have you experienced His provision spiritually, emotionally, and physically?

How generous are you in giving what you have been given? How well do you trust that he will continue to supply your needs?

How can you recognize and embrace God's promise of provision in times of scarcity or difficulty? Can you recall a time when God came through during a time of lack?

Reflect on a need you have today. How confident are you that God will prove Himself faithful in providing that need? How will you give what He provides back to Him by blessing someone else?

_____

_____

_____

_____

_____

_____

_____

_____

_____

_____

Why is it essential to have radical trust in God's provision for your own needs in order to be effectively used by Him to meet the needs of others?

_____

_____

_____

_____

_____

_____

_____

_____

_____

_____

CHAPTER 11

# CROSS WALKERS OF A NEW IDENTITY

The mandate is to follow Jesus and die to our selfish rebellion against God.

## READING TIME

As you read Chapter 11: "Cross Walkers of a New Identity" in *The Jesus Adventure,* review, reflect on, and respond to the text by answering the following questions.

# REVIEW, REFLECT, AND RESPOND

The chapter emphasizes walking in the new identity we have in Christ. How has your new identity changed you since you began following Jesus? What shifts have you noticed have taken place?

_____

_____

_____

_____

_____

In what areas of your life do you tend to seek your identity apart from God? How does that impact your relationship with Him?

_____

_____

_____

_____

_____

What are the key challenges that prevent you from fully embracing your new identity in Christ?

_____

_____

_____

_____

_____

_____

**THE JESUS ADVENTURE:** STUDY GUIDE | 75

> *"If any of you want to be my followers, you must forget about yourself. You must take up your cross and follow me."*
>
> —Mark 8:34 (CEV)

*Consider the scripture above and answer the following questions:*

How does denying ourselves make us more like God?

_____

_____

_____

_____

_____

_____

_____

What parts of yourself do you need to deny in order to fully follow Jesus?

_____

_____

_____

_____

_____

_____

_____

_____

How has your understanding of your identity in Christ evolved over time?

What does living your new identity look like in your relationships, career, and personal decisions? What does casting off your new identity look like?

How do you handle moments when your old self re-emerges? What are the warning signs that it is beginning to take over?

What kind of things do you say about yourself and the world that disagree with God's point of view? Make a list. What would God say about those things?

In what ways have you been reminded of your new identity in Christ when you felt it slipping away from your reality? Who has encouraged you, and what kind of shift took place?

Why is our old identity bondage, and what about our new identity gives us freedom?

CHAPTER 12

# THE TREASURE CHEST OF CHRIST

I believe that if we could see what is really awaiting us on the other side, we would willingly sacrifice everything and eagerly choose to be tortured for our faith in Jesus here.

## READING TIME

As you read Chapter 12: "The Treasure Chest of Christ" in *The Jesus Adventure*, review, reflect on, and respond to the text by answering the following questions.

# REVIEW, REFLECT, AND RESPOND

What kind of treasure is found in Christ?

_____

_____

_____

_____

_____

The author discusses accessing the treasures found in Christ through faith. What treasures do you think God has for you that you haven't yet discovered or received?

_____

_____

_____

_____

_____

What does it mean to store up more treasure in Heaven? What kind of things fall under that category?

_____

_____

_____

_____

_____

> *"But store up for yourselves treasures in heaven. . . . For where your treasure is, there your heart will be also."*
>
> —Matthew 6:20-21 (NIV)

*Consider the scripture above and answer the following questions:*

How does this scripture challenge you to reflect on where your heart and priorities lie?

_____

_____

_____

_____

_____

_____

_____

_____

Where have you stored up treasure? What are the warning signs that you are storing up earthly treasures? How can you begin to store up heavenly treasure through the filter of God's promises?

_____

_____

_____

_____

_____

_____

_____

_____

Who in your life bears the fruit of stored-up treasures on Earth? How is this influencing their character, joy, and relationship with Jesus?

_____

_____

_____

_____

_____

_____

Who in your life bears the fruit of stored-up treasures in Heaven? How is this influencing their character, joy, and relationship with Jesus?

_____

_____

_____

_____

_____

_____

_____

What kind of earthly treasures have you had to give up or sacrifice? What was that like for you, and how did it shape your walk with Jesus?

_____

_____

_____

_____

_____

_____

Which treasures that Christ has already given you are you most grateful for, and why? What other heavenly treasures are you seeking to receive from Him?

_____

_____

_____

_____

_____

_____

_____

The chapter highlights joy as a treasure of the Christian life. What is the difference between happiness and joy, and how can you cultivate more joy in your journey with Christ?

_____

_____

_____

_____

_____

_____

_____

What treasures do you feel God is calling you to pursue more intentionally as you continue in your adventure with Jesus?

_____

_____

_____

_____

_____

_____

_____